2020

Revisited

Shirlee Eskew Dashow

2020 Revisited

© 2021 Shirlee Eskew Dashow

ISBN PRINT 978-1-09836-400-7

DEDICATION

For my family who lived every day of 2020 with great courage.

TABLE OF CONTENTS

2020

Before

Long ago and far away;
Look careful, back, to the great before
Is there a way to find it;
It is there, the door

Before, we had professions;
Daily interaction at work
People were always around:
Some good, some bad, but an added perk

Before, there were life's choices:
Gym, bistro, cinema, trips, plans and more
Remember the friendships;
They were there before, the before

Before, our lives were changed:
We had no fear or dread
The door, ever ready to be opened;
But, now, it is lost, and we are dead

Pandemic

Is this truth or fallacy;
I step forward not knowing
Am I in the real world;
Or, do I not understand where I am going

Where did this all begin:
At first we were told, from
    bats in caves, or wet market stalls
We were trusting, were we not;
Now, it seems to have originated
    in China's scientific laboratory halls

Our country was shut down:
Some people became sick, some were dying
So many decisions had to be made fast:
Was our government telling us the truth,
    or lying

What to do, what precautions to take;
Do not have plans set, for they will change
Each day brings new scenarios and warnings:
Masks, sanitizers, distancing, treatments,
    death tallies and government orders we
    must rearrange

Pandemic;
It is here and our world will never
    be the same
Do, think or say what you will;
Covid-19 is its morbid name

Four Horsemen of the Apocalypse

Incoming to the present day;
They rode in hard, but will they stay
It depends on the state of man;
Will he fend them off, if he can

The first rides the steed of pandemic;
He is not particular about the disease endemic
It will spread as it will;
Our world, unprotected, it will kill

The second rides the steed of economic doom:
He spreads, wherever he goes, only panic and
    gloom
The people live in fear, mixed with spite and
    hate;
Waiting for the stimulus, hoping it won't be
    late

The third mounts the steed of racial division;
He hopes to run amok, without supervision
The cities are protesting, peaceful or not;
Humanity less human, this is our lot

The final mount is riding on the 2020
    elections;
He creates chaos with win and lose
    projections
The people must choose their coming
    fate;
Can they really change anything, or is it too
    late

People

We are all in this together;
The human race marching forward forever
Some think themselves better;
Perhaps they need a heads up, a letter

Dear, "Better Person" get down off your perch;
Others below you, left in the lurch
Come together now;
Working in unison somehow

Some want this, some that;
They had their swing, your turn to bat
Compromise is what is needed;
This philosophy must be heeded

People, we are just such;
Everyone must realize that much
With this decision;
We move forward with vision

Nominated

I stand before the people;
A Judge to be judged by all
The nomination to the highest court has come;
Now this woman will stand tall

Before a committee I must appear:
Their questioning will be long and grueling
Resolute, astute and knowledgeable
  I will come;
Ready for the Senate's dueling

This is a trial by fire;
The bi-partisan hatred is already apparent
I have come ready for their fight, not mine;
What they spew forth is aberrant

Questions and allegations will be thrown
  about:
In the end, I will not cave nor fall
They cannot make me someone I am not;
For a Judge among Judges must rise above all.

Words

Words have different meanings;
So, watch what you say
Good or bad leanings;
Depending on the day

A correct connotation to you;
May be opposite to another
What you say too;
Could be hurtful to some other

Words which stand alone;
Become different when together brought
Think about the tone;
Or the significance sought

Use your words well;
How important this is to see
What you say will tell:
Who you are and what you'll be

Election

Every four years, a Presidential Election:
An incumbent, or new selection
The right to choose:
One will win, one will lose

This right is a Constitutional protection;
One to prevent insurrection
No dictatorship to arise;
Freedom against false lies

A nation built on one hope;
That the great American experiment has
  scope
Looking toward selfless motivation;
To reconcile inclusive dedication.

May we continue on this road;
To stray, would strife unload
Let us remain undivided:
By rights, choices and freedoms guided

Election Rejection

An Election for President has come and gone;
The people have voted, had their say
Every four years this is mandated by law;
To make your choice is okay

But, this year, 2020, brought an
  unprecedented outcome:
One candidate declared victory,
  while the other will not concede
Here in lies the trickery;
Only one can lead

How does the nation proceed;
Two Presidents there cannot be
One must step forward, one back;
As soon as possible, let come the decree

There is the challenge of illegal votes;
Legal remedies are sought
Time is of the essence;
Decision must soon be brought

Our democracy is a wonder to behold;
It will move through inspection
Decisions will be made;
Honoring the system, using detection

At noon, on January 20, 2021;
Just one President will stand
Take the oath of office;
Confirm the greatness of our land

Quandary

Sitting at home with so much time;
What to do:

Read good books

Learn a new language on line

Go through old travel pictures for sake of
organization

Look through clothes for donation

Try out new recipes

Clean the house like never before

Write a verse or two, or more

Explore through closets, cupboards and drawers: what to throw and
what to keep

Call friends, and then call more friends

Send and receive texts and e-mails

Or, sit on the couch and stream

Or, just dream

Motherhood 2020

Mother, Oh Mother
She rises before the sun;
Up way before I have begun
Her life knows new change:
All is different and strange
There are no choices you see;
For a mother she will always be

Mother, Oh Mother
Life was easier before now;
For us she must triple her time somehow
She works two jobs every day;
This must be done for weekly pay
But, also, a teacher she must be;
To educate her children, we three

Mother, Oh Mother
After this she does elder care;
For grandma and grandpa, a wonderful pair
The house she cleans, the meals she makes:
Time she gives, and little she takes
She once was young, but now grows old;
A loving wonder to behold

Mother, Oh My Mother

Muscles

Sitting for so long;
The body forgets what a muscle is
Must try to work on muscle memory;
Give a body quiz

Like a couch, with memory foam;
It should restore to normal shape
This furniture looks good;
The body needs a visual drape

Perhaps, a trainer is the answer;
But, the gyms are closed right now
Then, learn, be a trainer;
Could possibly create a program
somehow

Ah, to think on this;
An answer will come
Meanwhile, this muscle memory;
Must try to be, not so dumb

Hibernation

Not a time for vacation
Not a reason for elation

First, came round one
Then, came two
Can you believe, now three

Round one was winter
Round two came spring
Now fall, we begin three

Surely, mistaken, this cannot be
Hibernation, is for bears you see

I am human, you cannot do this to me
You who are the powers that be

I am not meant to go to sleep for months:
Grow fat and have cubs

This is not humanity
Please, set me free

Travel

To take a trip would be fine:
A fantastic way to learn and spend time
What could be better:
Pack the suitcase and leave no letter

Take off to some exotic place;
Plan a bit, just in case
Sure to carefree be:
No time schedule, only free

This could be a plan;
It is possible, yes one can
Many places from which to choose:
Don't hesitate, don't lose

But wait, this cannot be done:
There are complications, not just one
Where to go, what places are open;
Places yes, but only token

Homeless

What happened, you are homeless, I am not;
Watching this closely from afar
Pondering this question;
Just who you are

Did you once have a home:
A family, a place to be
If so, where are they;
Please explain to me

But this won't happen now;
We are separate beings in time
Lives not intersecting:
You live yours, and I live mine

This situation is not right;
There must be a common ground
Some way to relate to one another;
Could not a plan be found

Food

Taken for granted, the food we eat;
There each day for the taking
One day this, next day that;
A project in the making

But, this is not the same for many;
Daily food is rare
Try as they might;
It is not always there

Why yes for me, but not thee;
Certainly not fair
To always have;
While you wait in despair

Take food to the Foodbank;
Quick, it is not too late
Take it now and often;
Please, don't wait

Ten Months and Counting

Ten months ago was normal life;
No call for strife
All in Bali was beauty, lush;
By the ocean, no need to rush
Then with haste came blame;
The world turned, no longer the same

People panicked overnight;
Barreling home in fright
Who was wrong, who was right;
Nations shutting down, uptight
Quarantine, if you care;
If not, beware

All, shut down to begin;
To not, is a sin
How long must we follow;
Normal life is but hollow
If different, you choose to be;
Powers that are will make you see

No need to be contrary;
Normal you know, is now scary
Ten months and counting, in a row:
No way out, no place to go
Tally the losses, comes to all;
Go ahead, they are not small

Shut in or not, it does not matter;
It is the same, the former or the latter

Unity

Unity is a kind and considerate word in
  meaning and purpose

To unify is to have a singleness of mind, or a
  mutual understanding of a common endpoint

Unity does not wander toward separateness
  or discord

To create such a state requires a concerted
  effort, of continual, meaningful compromise

Where is unity in today's world where people
  are polarized to opposite points of view:
There is only a push for the individual's right
  to bloviate, separate, but not renew

To continue in this concerted, continuity of
  non-peaceful, existence, is less than
  meaningless resistance:
This constant state of disconnectedness,
  a grating, disjointed song, leads not to a
  fullness of life, but to one only of subsistence

Is there not more to life than meager
  subsistence, working toward amalgamation
  and cooperation with our fellow human
  beings who walk this earth:
There being a dance of common courtesy,
  rather than constant consternation, one to
  fullness, one to dearth

Picture, not a world divided, but united,
  as people join together for communal good:
Where there is a shared effort toward
  civility and livability, loving one
  another as we should

"Can't we all just get along"

Family

My Love

My love and I;
A binding tie
There could be no other;
From day one, loving one another

First knew of him when young;
Before our love had begun
We both in orchestra played;
Was student conductor, he made

Did not admire him from afar;
Though, he thought himself a rising star
He only played second violin;
I played first, which was the win

Later, in high school, he did appear;
I signed up for Chemistry, oh dear
There, he at head table sat;
While, I remained in the back

Soon obvious, help was needed;
No problem, I succeeded
Looking around the class for the best;
There, he stood out among the rest

Now, all is just history;
It all began with chemistry
A bit of mine, a bit of his;
There our love began, and ever is

Siblings

One, two, three:
You, me and thee
We have shared our lives, we agree:
First one, then two, then three

Sister and brothers we decree;
From the same mother you see
However, so different we;
Raised alike, now free

One artistic, with creativity
Two scientific, came to be
Three, not sure, who is he;
Pure unknown, with glee

Life moves on for we three;
But, though unique, still close are we
Accepting the mark of family:
One, two and three

Rebe

Beautiful little one of mine;
You have grown-up with time
My treasure, my first born;
From innocence you have been torn
As parents we treated you so well;
The world was different, do tell

You were a beauty, inside and out:
Kind and giving to a fault, no doubt
So talented and artistic you see;
What should have been easy was not to be
You worked and struggled so hard;
Lady Luck was not your card

There were people who treated you cruel;
This was sad, but not the rule
Down for the count, you never gave in;
You clawed your way up to begin again
Your soul you never sold;
Your beauty, in and out, you did hold

So, my daughter, beautiful little one of mine;
You have gained a second chance in time

The Rebel

To be mine;
You did not choose
Born to be you;
The crooked path, or lose

Different from the start;
Not easy, confusing
Keeping sight of you;
Through life perusing

First here, then there;
Scattered, not slow
How to track;
Always on the go

Love, not an option;
God given child
Only a mother could follow;
This son so wild

Of well known fame;
Broke the rules many times over
Strayed far from home;
Why a hell bent rover

Searched the world;
Learned, tried it all
Then, brought all together;
Settled down, but on his call

The Rebel

Family

C

Came to us not long ago
  from across the oceans;
Bearing centuries of tradition
  and culture

As beautiful as the cherry blossoms
  that bloom in the spring;
And as strong as the wood of
  that tree

A deep current of fortitude
  within;
Driving this young woman
  to seeking and success

Different from us it
  seems;
But, yet, are we not all
  from the same human race

Much to impart,
  but much to learn;
Have we not shared
  in the bargain

Now, part of us,
  we travel on together:
This road of family
  and life

We welcome C

Pure Glee

A child come late;
Unknown, pure glee

An unexpected gift;
Better than any ever received

Adored by older, doting parents

Cared for by loving siblings

Surrounded by friends and family

Full of unbelievable, abundant joy

Made each day a wonderful adventure

His name is kindness

Can't ask why we were so blessed

Just too good to be;

This child come late, unknown, pure glee

Boo

Who is Boo;
Who are you
Is this the Boo;
As in Boo-hoo
Oh no, not you;
You are the magnificent Boo
There is only one like you;
The one and only Boo

One could try to replicate you;
But, not possible Boo
Only once can there be a Boo;
If you have one, lucky you
To have been given a Boo;
That was a Four Leaf Clover for you
A Boo will bring great joy too;
Please use this gift from Boo

He has the smart gene, that Boo;
Let it work well for you
He has the music gift, that Boo:
So, let him sing and play for you
He has the artistic eye, that Boo;
So, let him create for you
He can cook too, that Boo
Show him the kitchen, you

Oh Boo;
Who are you
The joy of my life;
That is who

Far to go

Iz, Av and Jo;
So very young
As of now, their lives are new;
Their paths unsung

Up in Alaska is home;
So far, but a great place to be
A land of wonders;
Open to adventure to you three

Ski, skate, fish, hunt, explore
   and so much more;
A pact with great living
When we visit, we learn so much:
A time for sharing and giving

Who knew just a few short years ago;
There would be a new tribe of five
So far away, yet always close;
In our hearts, ever near, and so alive

So, Iz, Av and Jo:
Watched and loved as you grow
Your lives new and unsung;
Will be great, this we know

Family

Autism

How to describe from afar;
This unusual behavior that leaves a scar
The individual resides alone;
Though surrounded by many, this is known

Common, interaction is not understood;
Natural instincts are not good
Entering new situations is felt traumatic;
Resulting movements become dramatic

Inside their mind, they are stuck;
Escaping this existence, is not their luck
The life you take for granted;
Is to them, a world slanted

The touch of humanity, is by most desired:
To them it is not wanted or required
Man is a creature who lives among many;
While the autistic person is fine without any

Their world we cannot enter:
Their feelings are their core and center
We can, hopefully, love them as they will be;
They are who they are, God's children, as we

Bubbie

Beneath the scarlet sky;
"Hi Bubbie"

Family

If you need us;
We are here
All for one;
One for all
If you need us;
We are near
All for one;
One for all

If we rise;
We rise together
All for one;
One for all
If we fall;
We fall whether
All for one;
One for all

So, if you need us;
We are here
All for one;
One for all

Just call

Moments

Joy

Can't buy it on the street,
Can't buy it at the store:
It is not something bought, or sought
It emanates from your soul

There

Where: the sun warms your face, leaves
crunch under foot, snowflakes melt on lashes,
rain piddles in puddles, rainbows appear,
pictures form in clouds and sun sets in glorious colors

Where: babies are born, pets love you, friends
hug, children laugh, people smile, lovers kiss,
help reaches the needy and the unexpected
happens

Where: the walk is brisk, cool air hits your
face, sand warms your feet, waves slap your
legs, kayak rolls gently, trail is hiked, fish jump
in stream, lake feels refreshing, mountain climb
is vigorous and body challenged

Where: home is near, door opens, dinner is
cooking, fire warms, greeting is loving,
conversation stimulates, phone doesn't
interrupt, book is open and bed is warm

Born

To be born is to die;
One comes before the other
You were there for my first cry;
Oh, my dear mother

One has but few years;
Growing old so soon
Years good, or with fears;
Life well lived, a boon

The cycle, fixed from first to last;
Focused on now, not the past
First, comes youth; spring
Fall, is what aging brings

If, past fall one goes;
They are in the winter pose
With winter comes the close;
Death being the final repose

To be born is to die

Life

The gift that keeps giving

Pure joy; a reason for thanksgiving

The baby, awakened to newness each day

The child, adorned by countless wonders

The youth, filled with thrills and mixed emotions

The adult, grown and seeking

The aged, content to just be

Oh life, whatever your mission; you have been a gift in transition

Thanks

Proper

What is proper;
What is just
Do what you do;
Or, do what you must

Rise each day to expectation;
Life is not, you know, a vacation
Ever moving forward;
But, what please, toward

One does this;
Strange to miss
Another does that;
Oh my, what scat

Noble and proper;
Please meet the mark
Heed whose warning;
On what chart

Silly

Silly, as only silly can be;
Willy nilly that's me
Life is way too serious;
It makes me quite delirious

Be silly when you choose;
See, nothing to lose
One can always serious be;
But, to be silly, is to be free

If, each day, there was no fun;
Why awake, or begin the begun
So happy to spread joy;
Just use silly as the ploy

Silly is as silly does;
Just rise up silly, just because
Don't let life pass you by;
Please, give silly a try

Taking a Walk

Down by the waterfront

The promise of a new venture

The body moving to the
rhythms of this given day

The sun's warmth on your face

The breeze to keep you cool
as your limbs work up a sweat

The waves beating against the shore,
giving a tempo to walk with

The liveliness of others around you

The children's unexpected
squeals of delight

The bikers, skateboarders, runners...

The dogs in the driftwood, digging

The laughter rising high,
all the way to heaven,
on wings of happiness

Just Taking a Walk

Sun

Rising each morning,
  light to all the world

Happiness, brought
  by its warmth

Missed, when it
  does not shine

An indication that life
  proceeds as normal:

As day follows night,
  so, the sun follows the
  moon

God's gift to man

Perfect fall morning

In Wright Park

Cross-country runners: team shirts, coaches
with stop watches, fans rooting

Foggy mists (foggy mornings, mean sunny
afternoons)

Dogs sprinting for balls and frisbees

Leaves deciding to fall

Chestnuts dropping; soon to be collected by ambitious cooks

A ghost visiting the swings of younger years

Normalcy still there; thank you God

Warmth

Warmth invades where man allows it to enter;
A need at the very core of his center

Physical warmth

I sit in the warmth of my home;
Surrounded by family, not alone
Thinking back to long ago;
When early man did not have it so
Just to have sun upon his face;
Was a warming grace
Sun, a daytime episode;
Turned night into cold

How then to manage this;
Shelter was not effortless
Moving boulders, rocks and trees;
A cave is found to appease
Conceptually, a revolution;
Moving upward in evolution
Cave habitation;
Improved man's situation

Still lacking enough warmth and light;
Led early man to new insight
Only by happenstance;
Flints rubbed together created chance
Spark to flame;
Life after, never the same
Fire, a source of imagination:
Man's celebration and jubilation

While skinning animals to cook;
The hides deserved a second look
Protection from weather while inside;
Led man to ponder the warmth of hide
This very foe he killed to eat;
Had its own protection from head to feet
Could not this animal insulation;
Change his clothing situation

Sun, shelter, fire and clothing;
Thank early man for purposing

WARMTH

Halloween

Each year, the end of October;
People get silly, raked over
Old and young, and inbetween;
Celebrate Halloween

They all dress to a tee;
Thousands of choices to be
Then on display, out they go;
Just to create quite the show

Youngsters will trick-or-treat;
Begging for candy to eat
Oldsters will get way too wild;
Party hearty like a child

All for creativity, and more;
Lots of surprises in store
Go out for spooky fun;
Once Halloween night has begun

Cooking

Let's take you where you've never been before;
So, he took me to the kitchen
Exactly correct, not for me;
Out quickly, quietly ditching

Then, shortly to return;
In need of a cup of tea
Did discover, quite by serendipity;
This place was for me

Oh dear, what turn of events;
Come for tea, but discover more
Looking for something to eat;
A few ingredients to score

Ingredients make nothing, alone;
If mixed, who knows
This was fun, this was joy;
Who could have known, or supposed

What combined together to have with tea;
Was really quite good
Now, the kitchen is a must;
Cooking, is a permanent should

Thanksgiving

Where is the turkey;
That gobbling bird should be in the oven
Yes, it is early;
But, the company is coming

Food to find and prepare;
Get it all out now
To cut, mix, bake and fix;
The end point, not when, but how

The table set, the chairs in place:
Then, hang the wreath, start the fire
The finest feast;
To this aspire

Hurry, change out of your jammies;
Put on something festive
While you're at it, mix the drinks;
No time to be restive

We have made it;
Think we are ready
Start the music, open the door:
Family and friends are here, be steady

Thanksgiving

The River

Sitting alone, by the river;
Gazing off to ponder
What lies ahead;
Around the bends, yonder

The water passes, flowing;
Forever moving, not smooth
Coming quickly, passing by;
No time to lose

Life is, as the river;
We wonder where it's going
Will our ride take us far;
Or the curves cause our slowing

Living pushes ever forward:
Halting and hurdling through each day
The moments, here then there;
We try, but we have no say

Musings

Adoption

Not knowing where you've been;
Not knowing where you're going
Alone onto yourself;
In the water, rowing

Now you see me;
Chosen from among many
What brought me to this place;
To be picked up like a lucky penny

Will I be kept or discarded;
Pennies are shiny when new
Will I grow dull from this process;
Or, perhaps develop a new hue

It is a tricky business;
But, had I another option
Stepping forward toward the choice;
Would I have chosen adoption

Laughter

Listen, it is
all around you

It is in the simple
joys that surround life

As children pass you,
it tinkles in your ears like bells

There, as two old friends
meet for a cup of...

Then, at the corner grocers,
as you enter the door

Heard, peeling off
church walls after services

Lifting softly up, as
two lovers drift slowly by

On your park path, as
runners race forward together

Passing you, as you
cross the crowded street

At your family
table, as you eat

Listen, to this
scintillating sound of life

Laughter

Purple

Color gives us blue and red;
Single colors, just so
But, then try purple instead;
A mix, much better you know

Are you blue or red bred;
You should mix it up
Blending both in your head;
Then life bears a full cup

There was a prince of Purple Rain;
Brilliant man, died too young
What did he teach us when he came;
To care about our brother, he sung

Another Prince did reign too;
He lived long ago, but preached to tame
Love your brother, as He loved you;
A man with passion He came

PURPLE

Wind through a Window

Look at nature's force

Waves with whitecaps,
tipping, bending

Plantings, bowing down,
rising, and bowing again to
the unrelenting push

Ships as big as buildings,
rocking to-and-fro,
up and down, back and forth

People bent forward
in walking struggle,
as if pushing cement

Wind chimes no longer tinkling,
become clanging, discordant bells

Inside, glad to be, observing
Wind through a Window

You are speaking to me, I presume

When you call me a Jesus Freak;
Someone mislead and weak
You are wrong;
I am not weak, but strong

Yes, I am Christian through and through;
Because He died for me and you
To me, you are my brothers:
I love you and all others

I stand tall for my belief;
Not growing weary is my relief
As Jesus gave his life for me;
I give mine to you, you see

So, when you call me a Jesus Freak;
Someone mislead and weak
You are wrong;
I am not weak, but strong

J and J

Janis and Jimi took the stage;
A music revolution
Their lives but short;
Heralded a societal evolution

Met them both in London Town:
When young and going round
Only twenty-one and free;
Free to be you, free to be me

Our world was changing:
Martin, John and Bobby died
Vietnam imploded;
The music spoke, "You lied".

The times brought turmoil;
To go back was not to be
Unfinished business then;
Has now shadowed you and me

When these years had passed by;
A new world order had begun
And, looking round, behind;
J and J had already sung

Listen to the Quiet

The peace of Quiet;
The silent whisper in the ear
The noise of no noise;
Resounds so dear

Can you hear the minute hum;
Of nothing in the air
Pause and note the vacuum;
If you will, if you dare

The cacophony of still;
One can hear this clatter
Back and forth, in the surround;
Until, sweetly, it does not matter

Blowing faintly through your hair;
In and out, out and in
There, so near, but far;
Whistling, the wind

See the waves, ascending heat;
Hear the silent warm
Rising up before your eyes;
Intense before the storm

My heart with soft sound;
Beats in rhythmic time
To sense the motion, life giving;
Is a message so fine

Oh, the peace of Quiet

Poetry

Is a literary work in the form of verse:
To be a poet, is to be blessed or cursed
If an idea is to be written down;
Straight forward please, don't fool around

Some verse, pleasing when read;
Leaves one wanting more, it's said
Other verse can be so confusing;
Nonsensical, a mad man's musing

To be a poet, is to be a romantic;
Sorry, don't mean to be pedantic
Sitting in clouds, quietly looking out
Sending code to heaven, no doubt

Verse is of melodic and lyrical bent;
Sometimes, to a musician sent
Poetry may wax and wane;
Composed in many forms, not the same

Fog and Smoke

Risen but no vision:
Only fog and smoke
To ponder, is this wisdom;
Or more likely, a bad joke

Fog marks the change of season;
Transition from summer to fall
While the smoke indicates fire;
This is the scientific call

Foggy mornings become sunny afternoons;
This is my resolution
Smoke drifts in from surrounding fires:
Causing sorrow and pollution

Mother Nature nurtures with her dense, moist
    fog;
We welcome the enveloping blanket after
    summer's heat
Yet, we turn our backs on the stench of fire:
With burning eyes, noses and throats, we
    retreat

Polish

What can it do for you:
All those scratches and bumps, subdue
Are you imbued with imperfection;
Those traits less desired, upon reflection

Let us examine from head to toe;
A full inspection, so you will know
Not everyone is capable of this;
Will not waste the time, some hiss

To begin, let us start with hair;
There is a polish called color, if you care
As for skin, if of wrong tone;
There is a polish called makeup for that zone

Are the eyes a disliked color for you;
There is a polish called contacts of
    a different hue
How about your nails or lashes;
There is polish called, fake, for such clashes

If the body needs a lift;
A plastic surgeon has the polish
    to give this gift
If you need to apologize for your shape;
There is a polish called a trainer who
    will change that scape

As you see, there is a polish for everything:
No reason to have a scratch, imperfection
    or ding
Why go through life without your polish magic;
Now, wouldn't that be absolutely tragic

However, have you the polish for a kind heart;
That might be the place to start
Or how about a new shine on your soul;
That would be a solid goal

And, while you're at it, give a polish to love;
That would be appreciated by all below and
    above
When there is humanity for one and all;
There will be no need for polish or recall

Journey

Take one, make one;
Don't stay home
Why would you do so;
You'll be alone

Life should not be solitary;
Burdens to share, don't alone carry
Spread out, reveal yourself:
Good for you and your health

So much to learn;
Take the turn
This world has much to impart;
Yearn to wander, make your start

A journey is but a road;
Make yours different, be bold
Seek out to travel, take hold;
It can't be done once old

Writing

Sitting quietly, in reflection;
Trying to gather thoughts
Slowly building toward recollection;
Moments of life, drawing lots

Which ones of importance

There are those deep, lost;
Ones hard to surface, bring
Rising slowly to memory;
Seeking for the bell to ring

Which ones lost then found

Why search for the deep;
Inside this computerized brain
Are these lost morsels:
Worth time and strain

Which ones make me who I am

If the thoughts come up;
Slowly, there, one by one
Writing will begin;
The process begun

Which ones purge the psyche

To write is to remain sane;
The brain too full of matter
Reaching for release;
From the state of, Mad Hatter

Which ones renew the self

If writing does not come;
Mania will become dread
Positive shutdown follows;
Then, the sleep of the dead

Which is the end

Challenge

If you would, challenge is good;
If something new, sample you should
Why not try, a chance to take;
Really, what difference will it make

The difference is a change of mind;
Pushed ahead, not behind
The physical, tested too;
Creates a singular you, anew

A person can sit in place;
Their whole life but waste
Or, they can make a transformation;
Stepping forward, toward modification

If you won't, then don't, the challenge take;
Why hassle yourself for change's sake
When to be common is normal, just so;
Don't change, too far to go

A Good Book

A good book, a feast like no other;
Begin, ready to discover

Many genre:

History
Science
Military
Religion
Biography
Autobiography
Novels
Mystery
Travel
Music

And more than these;
Make a list, please

Once a start is made;
The prospects cascade
A book here, a book there;
Soon, books everywhere

Then, to share ideas anew;
So many, not just a few
Perhaps, start a group;
Impart new knowledge, begin the loop

Once a person, does so endeavor;
The habit is difficult to sever
Imagine new concepts galore;
Open a book, see what's in store

To be without a book, beyond imagination;
Totally true, without exaggeration
Once a well read person appears;
To be without a book causes fears

It has been said, "Well read, is well feed".